LET'S SPEAK SPANISH!
A FIRST BOOK OF WORDS

VIKING
Published by the Penguin Group
Penguin Books USA Inc., 375 Hudson Street, New York, New York 10014, U.S.A.
Penguin Books Ltd, 27 Wrights Lane, London W8 5TZ, England
Penguin Books Australia Ltd, Ringwood, Victoria, Australia
Penguin Books Canada Ltd, 10 Alcorn Avenue, Toronto, Ontario, Canada M4V 3B2
Penguin Books (N.Z.) Ltd, 182–190 Wairau Road, Auckland 10, New Zealand

Penguin Books Ltd, Registered Offices: Harmondsworth, Middlesex, England

First published in 1993 by Viking, a division of Penguin Books USA Inc.

10 9 8 7 6 5 4 3 2 1

Adapted from *The Kids Can Press French & English Word Book,*
first published in Canada by The Kids Can Press, 1991
Translated by Arshes Anasal

Library of Congress Cataloging-in-Publication Data
Let's speak Spanish: a first book of words /
edited by Katherine Farris; illustrated by Linda Hendry.   p.   cm.
Summary: Labeled pictures in Spanish and English introduce
vocabulary for familiar objects and events, as well as
concepts such as colors, numbers and opposites.
I S B N 0 - 6 7 0 - 8 4 9 9 4 - 4
1. Spanish language—Vocabulary—Juvenile literature.
2. Spanish language—Textbooks for foreign speakers—English—
Juvenile literature.   [1. Spanish language—Vocabulary.]
I. Farris, Katherine. II. Hendry, Linda, ill.
PC4445.L48 1993   468.2'421—dc20   92-41736 CIP AC

Printed in Mexico   Set in Century Schoolbook

LET'S SPEAK SPANISH!

A FIRST BOOK OF WORDS

EDITED BY **KATHERINE FARRIS**

ILLUSTRATED BY **LINDA HENDRY**

VIKING

Bienvenidos a mi casa
Welcome to my house

las tejas
shingles

el techo
roof

el dormitorio
bedroom

la ventana
window

el pórtico
porch

la pared
wall

la sala de estar
living room

el sótano
basement

los escalones
front steps

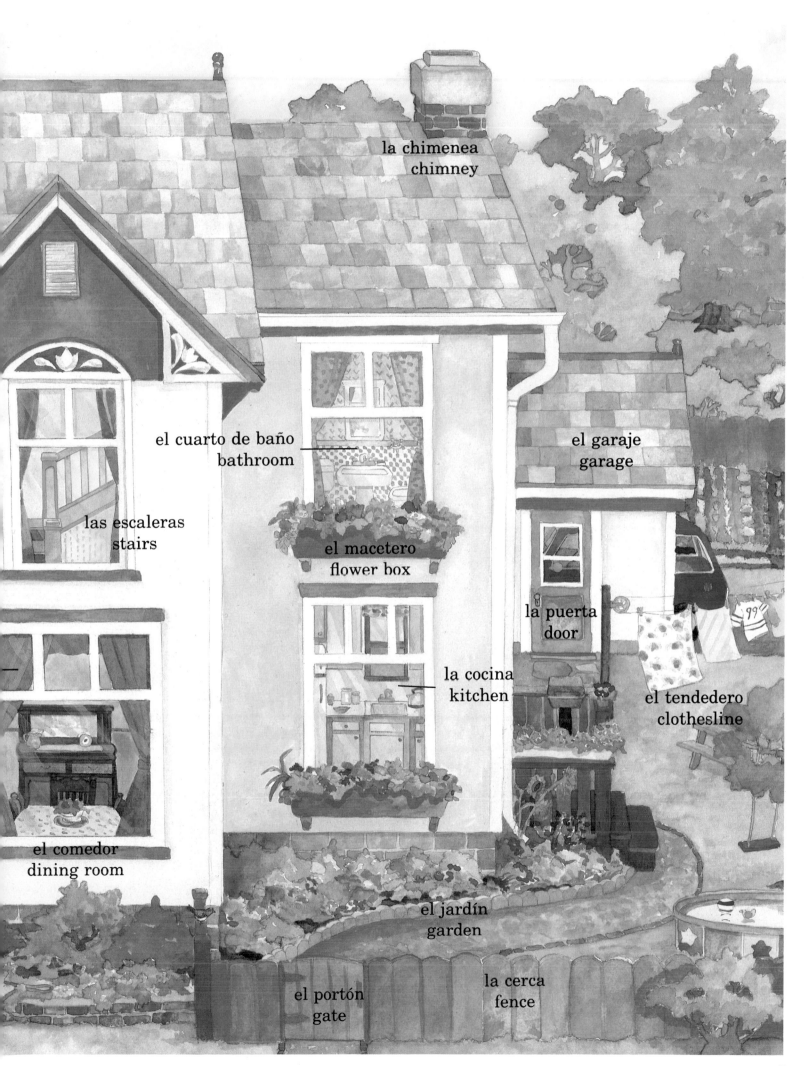

la chimenea
chimney

el cuarto de baño
bathroom

las escaleras
stairs

el macetero
flower box

el garaje
garage

la puerta
door

la cocina
kitchen

el tendedero
clothesline

el comedor
dining room

el jardín
garden

el portón
gate

la cerca
fence

Aquí está mi familia
Here's my family

el abuelo
grandfather

el primo
cousin

el papá
father

la prima
cousin

el hermano
brother

la mamá
mother

el bebé
baby

el perro
dog

la hermana
sister

6

la abuela
grandmother

la tía
aunt

el tío
uncle

la sobrina
niece

el sobrino
nephew

las mellizas
twins

el gato
cat

la bisabuela
great grandmother

el bisabuelo
great grandfather

Es de mañana
It's morning

cepillarse los dientes
brush your teeth

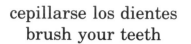

bañarse
take a bath

dormir
sleep

leer
read

sentarse
sit

freír un huevo
fry an egg

comer
eat

beber
drink

cortar el césped
mow the lawn

regar las plantas
water the plants

pelearse
fight

subir las escaleras
go up the stairs

ducharse
take a shower

secarse el pelo
dry your hair

planchar
iron

llorar
cry

caminar
walk

caerse
fall

reír
laugh

mirar televisión
watch TV

bajar las escaleras
go down the stairs

¡Buenos días!
Good morning!

la chaqueta
jacket

el sombrero
hat

la camisa
shirt

las botas
boots

los calcetines
socks

los zapatos
shoes

la bata de baño
bathrobe

el vestido
dress

los cordones
shoelaces

los zapatos deportivos
running shoes

la ropa interior
underwear

la camisa de entrenamiento
sweatshirt

la camiseta
T-shirt

la falda
skirt

los pantalones cortos
shorts

los pantalones
pants

el camisón
nightgown

el suéter
sweater

la gorra
hat

el chaleco
vest

el pijama
pajamas

el mitón
mitten

la bufanda
scarf

las pantuflas
slippers

el cinturón
belt

el abrigo
coat

11

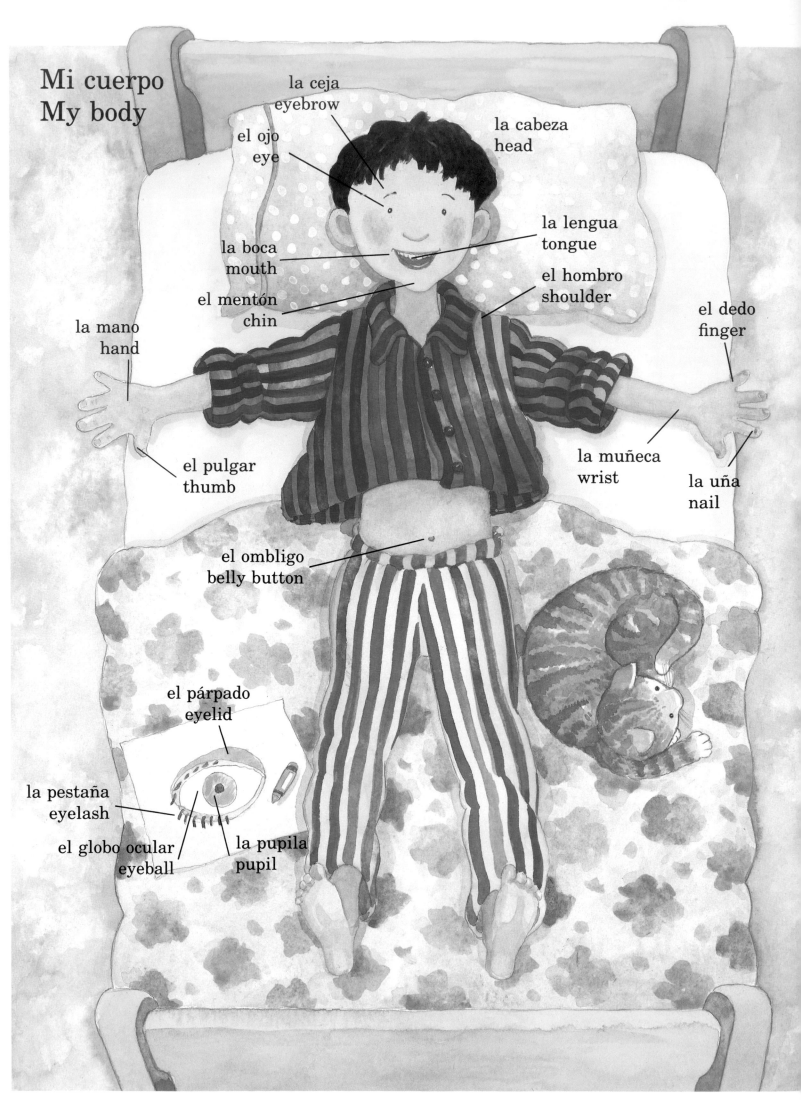

Mi cuerpo
My body

la ceja
eyebrow

el ojo
eye

la cabeza
head

la lengua
tongue

la boca
mouth

el hombro
shoulder

el mentón
chin

el dedo
finger

la mano
hand

el pulgar
thumb

la muñeca
wrist

la uña
nail

el ombligo
belly button

el párpado
eyelid

la pestaña
eyelash

el globo ocular
eyeball

la pupila
pupil

los ojos
eyes

el pelo
hair

el pelo castaño
brunette

la mejilla
cheek

la oreja
ear

el pelo rubio
blond

la nariz
nose

el diente
tooth

el cuello
neck

pelirrojo
rcdheaded

el codo
elbow

la espalda
back

el brazo
arm

la rodilla
knee

la pierna
leg

el dedo del pie
toe

el pie
foot

el tobillo
ankle

El desayuno
Breakfast time

el cuchillo
knife

el plato
plate

el tenedor
fork

la cuchara
spoon

la mantequilla
butter

los panecillos
rolls

la taza
cup

el huevo
egg

el azúcar
sugar

la tostada
toast

la tetera
teapot

la tostadora eléctrica
toaster

la leche
milk

el yogur
yogurt

el vaso de leche
glass of milk

el plátano
banana

las fresas
strawberries

el jugo de naranja
orange juice

la jarra
jug

el cereal
cereal

la manzana
apple

el tazón
bowl

el sándwich
sandwich

la mantequilla de cacahuate
peanut butter

En la escuela
At school

1 uno
2 dos
3 tres
4 cuatro
5 cinco
6 seis
7 siete

Hello
Bonjour
Hola

Buon giorno
Guten Tag

שלום
γειά σου
喂
こんにちは

la pizarra
blackboard

la maestra
teacher

el globo terráqueo
globe

el niño
boy

la niña
girl

el microscopio
microscope

los libros
books

el acuario
aquarium

el pez de colores
goldfish

el bate
de béisbol
baseball bat

el pupitre
school desk

los estudiantes
students

la jaula
cage

el libro
book

el hámster
hamster

el guante de béisbol
baseball mitt

16

ocho   nucve   diez

Bom dia
Goeden Dag
Goddag
Szerbusz

los planetas
planets

el reloj
clock

el conejo
rabbit

la marioneta
puppet

el almanaque
calendar

el mapa del mundo
map of the world

el piano
piano

el escritorio
desk

la guitarra
guitar

el sol
sun

el cesto de basura
garbage can

la trompeta
trumpet

la mochila escolar
school knapsack

la flauta
flute

el tambor
drum

los patines de rueda
roller skates

el juego
game

la pandereta
tambourine

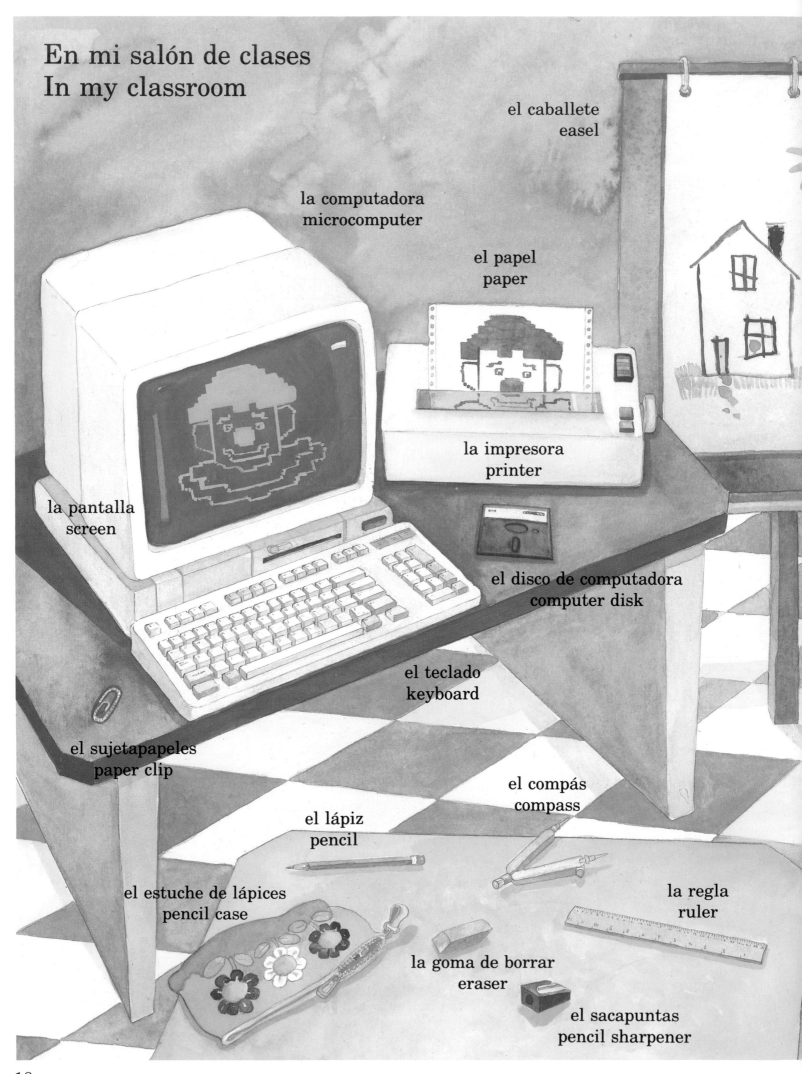

En mi salón de clases
In my classroom

el caballete
easel

la computadora
microcomputer

el papel
paper

la impresora
printer

la pantalla
screen

el disco de computadora
computer disk

el teclado
keyboard

el sujetapapeles
paper clip

el compás
compass

el lápiz
pencil

el estuche de lápices
pencil case

la regla
ruler

la goma de borrar
eraser

el sacapuntas
pencil sharpener

18

el dibujo
picture

la lata de pintura
can of paint

la caja de colores
paint box

los lápices de colores
colored pencils

los creyones
crayons

el pegamento
glue

el pincel
paintbrush

la cinta adhesiva
tape

las tijeras
scissors

el diccionario
dictionary

la calculadora
calculator

la pluma
pen

el libro de texto
textbook

1 + 1 = 2
1 + 2 = 3

el cuaderno
notebook

Lo que hago en la escuela
What I do at school

$$1 + 1 = 2$$
$$1 + 2 = 3$$
$$1 + 3 = 4$$

sumar
add

$$4 - 1 = 3$$
$$3 - 1 = 2$$
$$2 - 1 = 1$$

restar
subtract

dar de comer a los peces
feed the fish

contar
count

estudiar
study

jugar
play

columpiarse
swing

trepar
climb

correr
run

saltar a la cuerda
skip rope

escribir
write

pintar
paint

dibujar
draw

dormir la siesta
nap

21

Nos vamos de viaje
Going on a trip

el rascacielo
skyscraper

las nubes
clouds

la ciudad
city

el pueblo
village

el camino
road

el autobús escolar
schoolbus

el campo
field

el río
river

el zoológico
zoo

el espantapájaros
scarecrow

el establo
stable

el elefante
elephant

la jirafa
giraffe

el cisne
swan

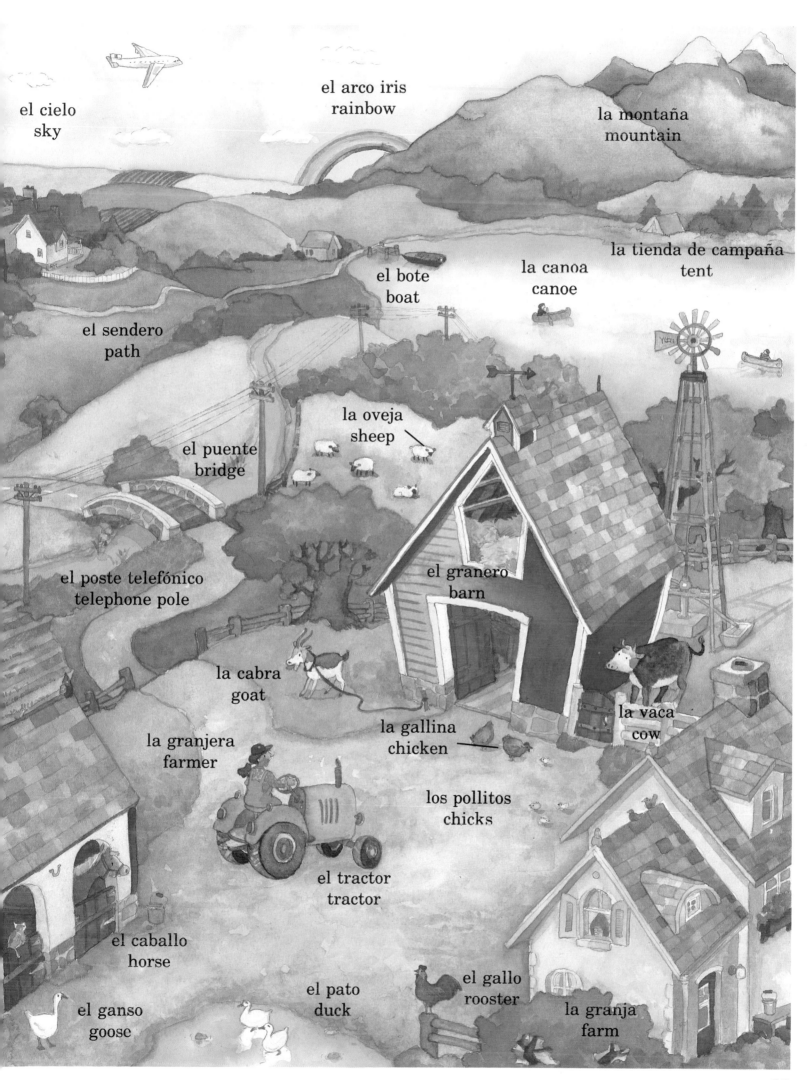

el cielo
sky

el arco iris
rainbow

la montaña
mountain

la tienda de campaña
tent

la canoa
canoe

el bote
boat

el sendero
path

la oveja
sheep

el puente
bridge

el granero
barn

el poste telefónico
telephone pole

la cabra
goat

la vaca
cow

la gallina
chicken

la granjera
farmer

los pollitos
chicks

el tractor
tractor

el caballo
horse

el gallo
rooster

el pato
duck

la granja
farm

el ganso
goose

En el zoológico
At the zoo

el respiradero
blowhole

la aleta
flipper

el delfín
dolphin

el caparazón
shell

la tortuga
tortoise

el hocico
snout

el jabalí
boar

el pico
beak

el ala
wing

el pájaro
bird

la piel
hide

la pluma
feather

la trompa del elefante
elephant's trunk

el colmillo del elefante
elephant's tusk

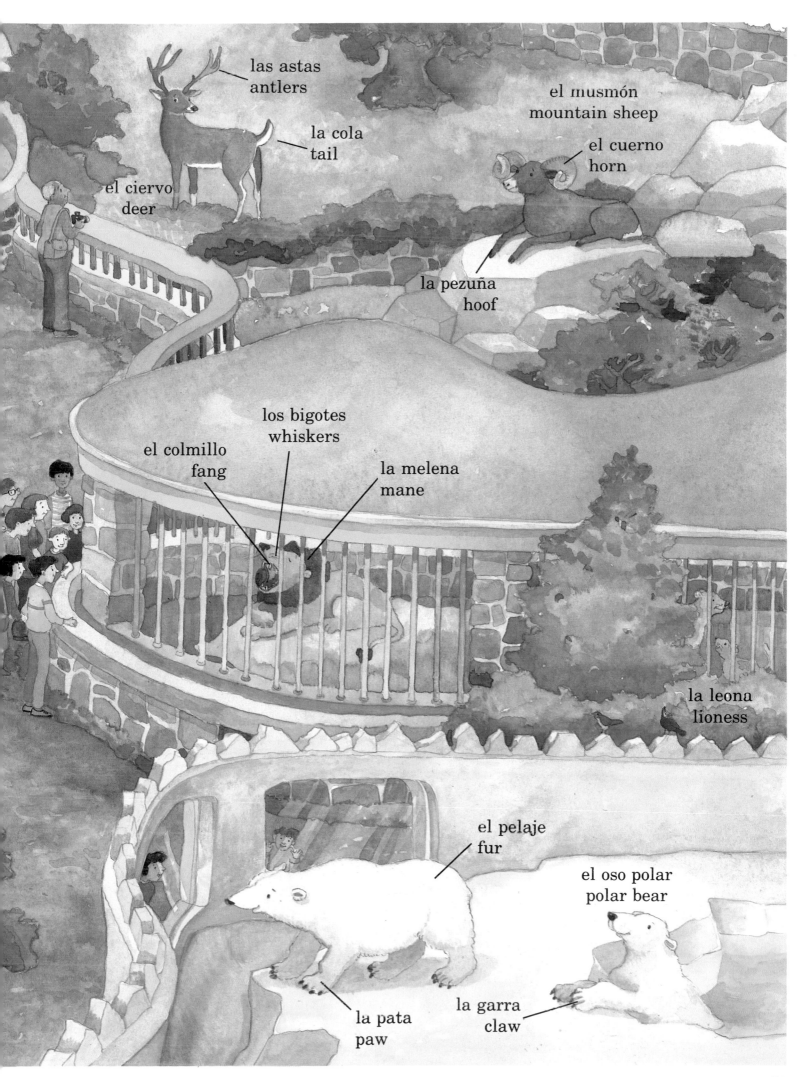

las astas
antlers

la cola
tail

el musmón
mountain sheep

el cuerno
horn

el ciervo
deer

la pezuña
hoof

los bigotes
whiskers

el colmillo
fang

la melena
mane

la leona
lioness

el pelaje
fur

el oso polar
polar bear

la pata
paw

la garra
claw

Mis animales favoritos del zoológico
My favorite zoo animals

el camello
camel

el flamenco
flamingo

la foca
seal

el hipopótamo
hippopotamus

el bisonte
bison

el canguro
kangaroo

el pingüino
penguin

el gorila
gorilla

la serpiente
snake

el mono
monkey

el tucán
toucan

el oso pardo
brown bear

el cocodrilo
crocodile

el ratón
mouse

el loro
parrot

el león
lion

el tigre
tiger

la ballena
whale

En la ciudad
In the city

el apartamento
apartment

el banco
bank

la peluquería
hairdresser

la librería
bookstore

el mural
mural

el hotel
hotel

la pescadería
fish store

la carnicería
butcher shop

la tienda de comestibles
grocery store

la acera
sidewalk

el taxi
taxi

la cabina telefónica
phone booth

el banco
del parque
park bench

el accidente
accident

el policía
police officer

el correo
post office

la fuente
fountain

el parque
park

el buzón
mailbox

la bandera
flag

el mástil de la bandera
flagpole

el hospital
hospital

la gran tienda
department store

el cuartel de bomberos
firchouse

el ciclista
cyclist

el restaurante
restaurant

la boca de incendios
fire hydrant

el cine
movie theater

el vendedor de flores
flower vendor

el peatón
pedestrian

el quiosco de periódicos
newsstand

el cruce de peatones
pedestrian crossing

la panadería
bakery

el letrero de la calle
street sign

En la tienda
At the store

la cajera
cashier

el apio
celery

la caja registradora
cash register

la bolsa de papel
paper bag

la clienta
customer

el plátano
banana

el limón
lemon

la piña
pineapple

el melocotón
peach

la manzana
apple

la naranja
orange

la toronja
grapefruit

la pera
pear

el albaricoque
apricot

la frambuesa
raspberry

la cereza
cherry

la ciruela
plum

el mango
mango

la sandía
watermelon

30

las uvas
grapes

el aguacate
avocado

la lechuga
lettuce

los guisantes
peas

el pepino
cucumber

el tendero
grocer

el tomate
tomato

la zanahoria
carrot

la cebolla
onion

la papa
potato

el maíz
corn

las judías verdes
green beans

Medios de transporte
Means of transportation

la ambulancia
ambulance

el helicóptero
helicopter

el cohete
rocket

el satélite
satellite

el barco de vapor
steamship

el velero
sailboat

el barco de motor
motor boat

el windsurf
windsurfer

el triciclo
tricycle

el automóvil deportivo
sportscar

el camión de auxilio
tow truck

el camión
truck

el jet
jet

el avión
plane

el autobús
bus

el tren
train

la bicicleta
bicycle

el carrito
wagon

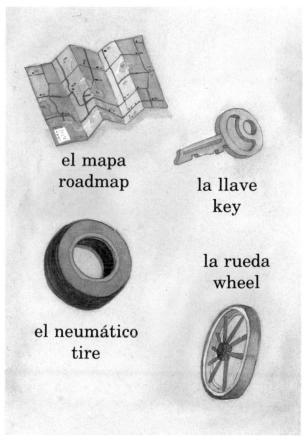

el mapa
roadmap

la llave
key

el neumático
tire

la rueda
wheel

el camión de repartos
delivery truck

el remolque
trailer

la casa rodante
motor home

En el jardín de mi casa
In my backyard

el balde
pail

la pala
shovel

el rastrillo
rake

la sombrilla de jardín
garden umbrella

el cajón de arena
sandbox

el diente de león
dandelion

la silla de jardín
garden chair

la patineta
skateboard

el geranio
geranium

la mariposa
butterfly

la libélula
dragonfly

la hormiga
ant

la mosca
fly

la terraza
deck

la barbacoa
barbecue

el carbón
charcoal

34

la golondrina
swallow

la hoja
leaf

la cortadora de césped
lawnmower

el árbol
tree

el columpio
swing

el césped
grass

la ardilla
squirrel

el pensamiento
pansy

la abeja
bee

la seta
mushroom

la violeta
violet

el girasol
sunflower

el petirrojo
robin

la rosa
rose

Barbacoa
Barbecue time

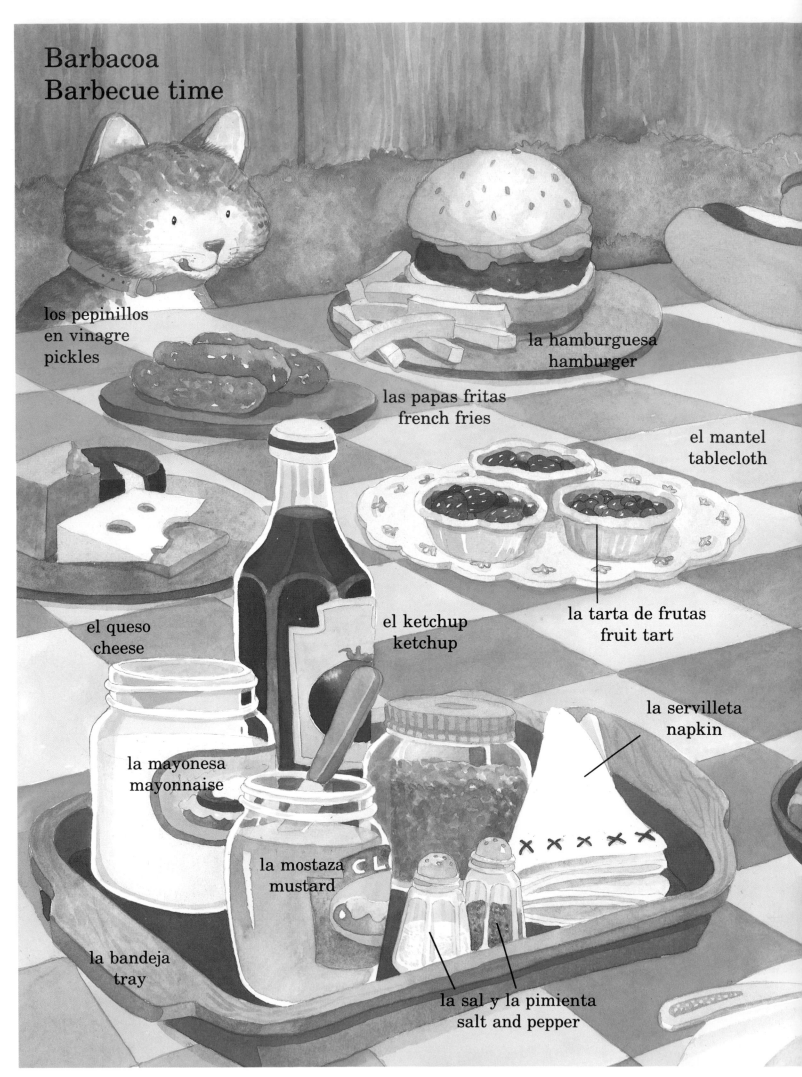

los pepinillos
en vinagre
pickles

la hamburguesa
hamburger

las papas fritas
french fries

el mantel
tablecloth

el queso
cheese

el ketchup
ketchup

la tarta de frutas
fruit tart

la servilleta
napkin

la mayonesa
mayonnaise

la mostaza
mustard

la bandeja
tray

la sal y la pimienta
salt and pepper

los perros calientes
hot dogs

el helado
ice cream

la torta
cake

la cesta de frutas
basket of fruit

la ensalada
salad

la gaseosa
soda pop

la mesa
table

las galletas
cookies

la ensalada de frutas
fruit salad

el jugo de fruta
fruit juice

Mis colores favoritos
My favorite colors

rosado
pink

anaranjado
orange

rojo
red

marrón
brown

negro
black

verde
green

castaño
beige

amarillo
yellow

azul
blue

gris
gray

morado
purple

blanco
white

Desde mi ventana
From my window

la estrella
star

la casa
house

la piscina
pool

el mapache
raccoon

la escalera
ladder

el cochecito del bebé
stroller

la casa en el árbol
treehouse

la acera
sidewalk

la luna
moon

el faro
headlight

el carro
car

el zorrillo
skunk

los amigos
friends

la iglesia
church

el murciélago
bat

la fuente
para los pájaros
birdbath

la parada del autobús
bus stop

el borde de la acera
curb

el nido
nest

la calle
street

la sombra
shadow

el búho
owl

41

¡Buenas noches!
Good night!

la persiana
blind

el florero
flower vase

el dibujo
picture

los padres
parents

la lámpara
lamp

la cama
bed

la sábana
sheet

el reloj despertador
alarm clock

la manta
blanket

el cajón
drawer

la cómoda
chest of drawers

las almohadas
pillows

la alfombra
carpet

el cepillo para el pelo
hair brush

la silla
chair

la radio
radio

la repisa
para libros
bookshelf

el tocadiscos
record player

el disco
record

los juguetes
toys

la pelota
ball

el espejo
mirror

el cepillo de dientes
toothbrush

el lavabo
sink

el jabón
soap

la ducha
shower

la toalla
towel

la bañera
bathtub

el inodoro
toilet

la alfombra del baño
bathmat

el peine
comb

el móvil
mobile

el osito de juguete
teddy bear

43

¿Cuál es el opuesto?
What's the opposite?

alto
high

cuadrado
square

redondo
round

bajo
low

sobre
on

debajo
under

frío
cold

caliente
hot

lleno
full

vacío
empty

blando
soft

duro
hard

seco
dry

mojado
wet

limpio
clean

sucio
dirty

abierto
open

cerrado
closed

grande
big

pequeño
small

feliz
happy

triste
sad

▶A
abeja *ah-BAY-ha*
abierto *ah-bee-AIR-toh*
abrigo *ah-BREE-go*
abuela *ah-BWAY-la*
abuelo *ah-BWAY-lo*
accidente *ahk-see-DEN-tay*
acera *ah-SEH-ra*
acuario *ah-KWAR-ee-o*
aguacate *uh-gwa-KAH-tay*
ala *AH-la*
albaricoque *ahl-bah-ree-KOH-kay*
aleta *ah-LEH-ta*
alfombra (del baño) *ahl-FOAM-bra (del BAHN-yo)*
almacén *ahl-mah-SEN*
almanaque *ahl-mah-NAH-kay*
almohadas *ahl-moh-AH-das*
alto *AHL-toh*
amarillo *ah-mah-REE-yo*
ambulancia *ahm-boo-LAHN-see-a*
amigos *ah-MEE-gos*
anaranjado *ah-nah-rahn-HAH-doh*
apartamento *ah-par-tah-MEN-toh*
apio *AHP-ee-o*
Aquí está mi familia *ah-KEE ehs-TA mee fah-MEEL-ee-ya*
árbol *AR-bohl*
arco iris *AR-ko EER-ees*
ardilla *ar-DEE-ya*
astas *AHS-tahs*
autobús (escolar) *ow-toh-BOOS (es-koh-LAR)*
automóvil deportivo *ow-toh-MOH-veel deh-por-TEE-vo*
avión *ah-vee-OHN*
azúcar *ah-SOO-kar*
azul *ah-SOOL*

▶B
bajar las escaleras *bah-HAR lahs es-kah-LAIR-as*
bajo *BAH-ho*
balde *BAHL-day*
ballena *bah-YEH-na*
bañarse *bahn-YAR-say*
banco (del parque) *BAHN-ko (del PAR-kay)*
bandeja *bahn-DEH-ha*
bandera *bahn-DEH-ra*
bañera *bahn-YEH-ra*
barbacoa *bar-bah-KO-a*
barco de motor *BAR-ko deh moh-TOR*
barco de vapor *BAR-ko deh vah-POR*
bata de baño *BAH-ta day BAHN-yo*
bate de béisbol *BAH-teh deh BASE-bohl*
bebé *beh-BEH*
beber *beh-BAIR*
bicicleta *bee-see-KLEH-ta*
Bienvenidos a mi casa *bee-en-veh-NEE-dohs ah mee KAH-sa*
bigotes *bee-GOH-tess*
bisabuela *bees-ah-BWAY-la*
bisabuelo *bees-ah-BWAY-lo*
bisonte *bee-SOHN-teh*
blanco *BLAHN-ko*
blando *BLAHN-doh*
boca (de incendios) *BOH-ka (deh een-SEN-dee-os)*
bola *BOH-la*
bolsa de papel *BOHL-sa deh pah-PEL*

borde de la acera *BORE-deh deh lah ah-SEH-ra*
botas *BOH-tas*
bote *BOH-tay*
brazo *BRAH-so*
Buenas noches *BWEH-nas NOH-chess*
Buenos días *BWEH-nohs DEE-ahs*
bufanda *boo-FAHN-da*
búho *BOO-o*
buzón *boo-SOHN*

▶C
caballete *kah-bah-YEH-tay*
caballo *kah-BAH-yo*
cabeza *kah-BAY-sa*
cabina telefónica *kah-BEE-na teh-leh-FOH-nee-ka*
cabra *KAH-bra*
caerse *kah-YAIR-say*
caja de colores *KAH-ha deh koh-LOH-rehss*
caja registradora *KAH-ha reh-hee-stra-DOR-a*
cajera *kah-HEH-ra*
cajón (de arena) *kah-HONE (deh ah-RAIN-a)*
calcetines *kahl-seh-TEEN-ess*
calculadora *kahl-koo-lah-DOR-a*
caliente *kahl-ee-EN-tay*
calle *KAH-yay*
cama *KAH-ma*
camello *kah-MEH-yo*
caminar *kah-mee-NAR*
camino *kah-MEE-no*
camión (de auxilio) *kah-mee-OHN (deh owk-SEEL-ee-o)*
camión de repartos *kah-mee-OHN deh reh-PAR-toss*
camisa (de entrenamiento) *kah-MEE-sa (deh en-tray-nah-mee-EN-toh)*
camiseta *kah-mee-SET-a*
camisón *kah-mee-SONE*
campo *KAHM-po*
canguro *kahn-GOO-ro*
canoa *kah-NO-a*
caparazón *kah-par-ah-SONE*
carbón *kar-BOHN*
carnicería *kahr-nee-ser-EE-a*
carrito *kah-RREE-toh*
carro *KARR-o*
casa *KAH-sa*
casa en el árbol *KAH-sa en el AR-bohl*
casa rodante *KAH-sa roh-DAHN-tay*
castaño *kah-STAHN-yo*
cebolla *seh-BOY-ya*
ceja *SEH-ha*
cepillarse los dientes *seh-pee-YAR-say lohs dee-EN-tess*
cepillo de dientes *seh-PEE-yo deh dee-EN-tess*
cepillo para el pelo *seh-PEE-yo PAH-ra el PEH-loh*
cerca *SAIR-ka*
cereal *seh-ray-AL*
cereza *seh-REH-sa*
cerrado *seh-RRAH-doh*
césped *SES-ped*
cesta de frutas *SES-ta deh FROO-tas*
cesto de basura *SES-toh deh bah-SOO-ra*
chaleco *chah-LAY-ko*

chaqueta *chah-KEH-ta*
chimenea *chee-meh-NAY-a*
ciclista *see-KLEE-sta*
cielo *see-EHL-o*
ciervo *see-EHR-vo*
cinco *SINK-o*
cine *SEE-nay*
cinta adhesiva *SEEN-ta ahd-heh EEV-a*
cinturón *seen-too-ROHN*
ciruela *see-roo-EH-la*
cisne *SEES-nay*
ciudad *see-yoo-DAHD*
clienta *klee-EN-ta*
cochecito del bebé *koh-chay-SEE-toh del beh-BEH*
cocina *koh-SEE-na*
cocodrilo *koh-koh-DREE-loh*
codo *KOH-doh*
cohete *koh-HEH-tay*
cola *KOH-la*
colmillo (del elefante) *kohl-MEE-yo (del eh-leh-FAHN-tay)*
columpiarse *koh-loom-pee-AR-say*
columpio *koh-LOOM-pee-o*
comedor *koh-meh-DOR*
comer *koh-MAIR*
cómoda *KOH-moh-da*
compás *kohm-PAHS*
computadora *kohm-poo-tah-DOR-a*
conejo *koh-NAY-ho*
contar *kohn-TAR*
cordones *kor-DOE-ness*
correo *koh-RREH-o*
correr *koh-RREHR*
cortadora de césped *kor-tah-DOR-a deh SES-ped*
cortar el césped *kor-TAR el SES-ped*
creyones *kray-OHN-ess*
cruce de peatones *KROO-say deh pay-ah-TOHN-ess*
cuaderno *kwah-DAIR-no*
cuadrado *kwah-DRAH-doh*
Cuál es el opuesto *kwal es el oh-PWES-toh*
cuartel de bomberos *kwar-TEHL deh bohm-BEH-ros*
cuarto de baño *KWAR-toh deh BAHN-yo*
cuatro *KWAH-tro*
cuchara *koo-CHAR-a*
cuchillo *koo-CHEE-yo*
cuello *KWAY-yo*
cuerno *KWER-no*

▶D
dar de comer a los peces *dar deh koh-MAIR ah lohs PEH-sess*
debajo *deh-BAH-ho*
dedo (del pie) *DEH-doh (del pee-AY)*
delfín *dehl-FEEN*
desayuno *des-eye-OON-o*
Desde mi ventana *DEZ-day mee ven-TAH-na*
dibujar *dee-boo-HAR*
dibujo *dee-BOO-ho*
diccionario *deek-see-oh-NAR-ee-o*
diente *dee-EN-tay*
diente de león *dee-EN-tay deh lay-OHN*
diez *dee-ESS*
disco (de computadora) *DEES-ko (deh kohm-poo-tah-DOR-a)*

dormir (la siesta)   *dor-MEER (lah see-EHS-ta)*
dormitorio   *dor-mee-TOR-ee-o*
dos   *dohs*
ducha   *DOO-cha*
ducharse   *doo-CHAR-say*
duro   *DOO-ro*

▶E
el   *ell*
elefante   *ehl-eh-FAHN-tay*
En el jardín de mi casa   *en el har-DEEN deh mee KAH-sa*
En el zoológico   *en el soh-oh LOH-hee-ko*
En la ciudad   *en lah see-yoo-DAHD*
En la escuela   *en lah es-KWAY-la*
En la tienda   *en lah tee-EN-da*
En mi salón de clases   *en mee sah-LONE deh KLAHS-ess*
ensalada (de frutas)   *en-sah-LAH-da (deh FROO-tas)*
escalera(s)   *es-kah-LEH-ra(s)*
escalones   *es-kah-LONE-ess*
escribir   *es-kree-BEER*
escritorio   *es-kree-TOR-ee-o*
Es de mañana   *es deh mah-NYAH-na*
espalda   *es-PAHL-da*
espantapájaros   *es-pahn-ta-PA-ha-ross*
espejo   *es-PEH-ho*
establo   *es-TAH-blo*
estrella   *es-TREH-ya*
estuche de lápices   *es-TOO-che deh LAH-pee-sess*
estudiantes   *es-too-dee-AHN-tess*
estudiar   *es-too-dee-AR*

▶F
falda   *FAHL-da*
faro   *FAR-oh*
feliz   *feh-LEASE*
flamenco   *flah-MAIN-ko*
flauta   *FLAOW-ta*
florero   *flor-EH-ro*
foca   *FOH-ka*
frambuesa   *frahm-BWAY-sa*
freír un huevo   *fray-EER oon WAY-vo*
fresas   *FREH-sas*
frío   *FREE-o*
fuente (para los pájaros)   *FWEN-tay (PAH-ra lohs PAH-hah-ross)*

▶G
galletas   *gah-YEH-tas*
gallina   *gah-YEE-na*
gallo   *GAH-yo*
ganso   *GAHN-so*
garaje   *gah-RAH-hey*
garra   *GARR-a*
gaseosa   *gah-seh-OH-sa*
gato   *GAH-toh*
geranio   *heh-RAH-nee-o*
girasol   *hee-rah-SOHL*
globo ocular   *GLO-bo oak-oo-LAR*
globo terráqueo   *GLO-bo teh-RRAH-kay-o*
golondrina   *goh-lohn-DREE-na*
goma de borrar   *GOH-ma deh bo-RRAR*
gorila   *goh-REE-la*
gorra   *GORR-a*
grande   *GRAHN-day*
granero   *grahn-EH-ro*
granja   *GRAHN-ha*
granjera   *grahn-CHAIR-a*
gran tienda   *grahn tee-EN-da*
gris   *grease*

guante de béisbol   *GWAHN-teh deh BASE-bohl*
guisantes   *ghee-SAHN-tess*
guitarra   *ghee-TARR-a*

▶H
hamburguesa   *ahm-boor-GAY-sa*
hámster   *AHM-ster*
helado   *eh-LAH-doh*
helicóptero   *el-ee-KOHP-teh-ro*
hermana   *air-MAH-na*
hermano   *air-MAH-no*
hipopótamo   *ee-poh-POH-tah-mo*
hocico   *oh-SEE-ko*
hoja   *OH-ha*
hombro   *OHM-bro*
hormiga   *or-MEE-ga*
hospital   *ohs-pee-TAHL*
hotel   *oh-TEL*
huevo   *WAY-vo*

▶I
iglesia   *ee GLEH-see-a*
impresora   *eem-preh-SOAR-a*
inodoro   *een-oh-DOR-o*

▶J
jabalí   *hah-bah-LEE*
jabón   *ha-BOHN*
jardín   *har-DEEN*
jarra   *HARR-a*
jaula   *HAOW-la*
jet   *jet*
jirafa   *hee-RAH-fa*
judías verdes   *hoo-DEE-as VER-dess*
juego   *HWAY-go*
jugar   *hoo-GAR*
jugo de fruta   *HOO-go deh FROO-ta*
jugo de naranja   *HOO-go deh nah-RAHN-ha*
juguetes   *hoo-GEH-tess*

▶K
ketchup   *KEH-choop*

▶L
la   *lah*
lámpara   *LAHM-pah-ra*
lápices de colores   *LAH-pee-sess deh koh-LOH-rehss*
lápiz   *LAH-peace*
las   *lahs*
lata de pintura   *LAH-ta deh peen-TOO-ra*
lavabo   *lah-VAH-bo*
leche   *LAY-chay*
lechuga   *leh-CHOO-ga*
leer   *lay-AIR*
lengua   *LEN-gwa*
león   *lay-OHN*
leona   *lay-OHN-a*
letrero de la calle   *leh-TREH-ro deh lah KAH-yay*
libélula   *lee-BEH-loo-la*
librería   *lee-breh-REE-a*
libro (de texto)   *LEE-bro (deh TEKS-toh)*
limón   *lee-MOHN*
limpio   *LEEM-pee-o*
llave   *YAH-vay*
lleno   *YEH-no*
llorar   *yor-AR*
Lo que hago en la escuela   *lo kay AH-go en lah es-KWAY-la*
loro   *LORE-oh*
los   *lohs*
luna   *LOO-na*

▶M
macetero   *mah-seh-TEH-ro*
maestra   *mah-EHS-stra*
maíz   *mah-YEES*
mamá   *mah-MA*
mango   *MAHN-go*
mano   *MAH-no*
manta   *MAHN-ta*
mantel   *mahn-TELL*
mantequilla (de cacahuate)   *mahn-teh-KEE-ya (deh kah-kah-WAH-teh)*
manzana   *mahn-SAH-na*
mapa (del mundo)   *MAH-pa (del MOON-doh)*
mapache   *mah-PAH-chay*
marioneta   *mah-ree-ohn-ET-a*
mariposa   *mah-ree-POH-sa*
marrón   *mah-RROHN*
mástil de la bandera   *MAHS-teel deh lah bahn-DEH-ra*
mayonesa   *mah-yohn-EH-sa*
Medios de transporte   *MEH-dee-ohs deh trahns-POHR-tay*
mejilla   *meh-HEE-ya*
melena   *meh-LEH-na*
mellizas   *meh-YEES-as*
melocotón   *meh-loh-koh-TOHN*
mentón   *men-TONE*
mesa   *MEH-sa*
microscopio   *mee-kroh-SKOH-pee-o*
Mi cuerpo   *mee KWER-po*
mirar televisión   *meer-AR teh-leh-vis-YONE*
Mis animales favoritos del zoológico   *mees ah-nee-MAH-less fah-vor-EE-tos del soh-oh-LOH-hee-ko*
Mis colores favoritos   *mees koh-LOH-rehss fah-vor-EE-tohs*
mitón   *mee-TONE*
mochila escolar   *moh-CHEE-la es-koh-LAR*
mojado   *moh-HA-doh*
mono   *MOH-no*
montaña   *mohn-TAHN-ya*
morado   *moh-RAH-doh*
mosca   *MOH-ska*
mostaza   *moh-STAH-sa*
móvil   *MOH-veel*
muñeca   *moon-YEH-ka*
mural   *moo-RAHL*
murciélago   *moor-see-EL-ah-go*
musmón   *moose-MOHN*

▶N
naranja   *nah-RAHN-ha*
nariz   *nah-REES*
negro   *NEH-gro*
neumático   *nay-oo-MAH-tee-ko*
nido   *NEE-doh*
niña   *NEE-nya*
niño   *NEE-nyo*
Nos vamos de viaje   *nohs VAH-mohs deh vee-AH-hay*
nubes   *NOO-bess*
nueve   *NWAY-vay*

▶O
ocho   *OH-cho*
ojo(s)   *OH-ho(s)*
ombligo   *ohm-BLEE-go*
oreja   *oar-RAY-ha*
osito de juguete   *oh-SEE-toh deh hoo-GEH-teh*
oso pardo   *OH-so PAR-doh*

oso polar *OH-so poh-LAR*
oveja *oh-VAY-ha*
▶**P**
padres *PAH-drehs*
pájaro *PAH-ha-ro*
pala *PAH-la*
panadería *pah-nah-deh-REE-a*
pandereta *pahn-deh-REH-ta*
panecillos *pah-nay-SEE-yohs*
pantalla *pahn-TIE-ya*
pantalones (cortos) *pahn-tah-LONE-ess
  (KOR-tohs)*
pantuflas *pahn-TOO-flas*
papá *pah-PAH*
papa *PAH-pah*
papas fritas *PAH-pahs FREE-tahs*
papel *pah-PEHL*
parada del autobús *pah-RAH-da del
  ow-toh-BOOS*
pared *pah-RED*
párpado *PAR-pah-doh*
parque *PAR-kay*
pata *PAH-ta*
patines de rueda *pah-TEE-ness deh roo-
  EH-da*
patineta *pah-tee-NEH-ta*
pato *PAH-toh*
peatón *pay-ah-TONE*
pegamento *peh-gah-MEN-toh*
peine *PAY-neh*
pelaje *peh-LAH-heh*
pelearse *peh-leh-AR-say*
pelirrojo *peh-lee-RROH-ho*
pelo (castaño) *PEH-lo (ka-STAHN-yo)*
pelo rubio *PEH-lo ROO-bee-o*
pelota *peh-LOH-tah*
peluquería *peh-loo-keh-REE-a*
pensamiento *pen-sah-mee-EN-toh*
pepinillos en vinagre *peh-pee-NEE-yos
  en vee-NAH-gray*
pepino *peh-PEE-no*
pequeño *peh-KEHN-yo*
pera *PEH-ra*
perro *PERR-o*
perros calientes *PERR-os
  kahl-ee-YEN-tess*
persiana *per-see-AH-na*
pescadería *pes-kah-der-EE-a*
pestaña *pes-TAHN-ya*
petirrojo *peh-tee-RROE-ho*
pez de colores *pes deh koh-LOH-rehss*
pezuña *pehs-OON-ya*
piano *pee-AH-no*
pico *PEE-ko*
pie *pee-AY*
piel *pee-EL*
pierna *pee-AIR-na*
pijama *pee-HAH-ma*
piña *PEE-nya*
pincel *peen-SEHL*
pingüino *peen-GWEE-no*
pintar *peen-TAR*
piscina *pee-SEE-na*
pizarra *pee-SAH-rra*
planchar *plahn-CHAR*
planetas *plah-NEH-tas*
plátano *PLAH-tah-no*
plato *PLAH-toh*
pluma *PLOO-ma*
policía *poh-lee-SEE-a*
pollitos *poh-YEE-tos*

pórtico *POR-tee-ko*
portón *por-TONE*
poste telefónico *POH-stay
  teh-leh-FOH-nee-ko*
prima *PREE-ma*
primo *PREE-mo*
pueblo *PWEB-lo*
puente *PWEN-tay*
puerta *PWER-ta*
pulgar *pool-GAR*
pupila *POO-pee-la*
pupitre *poo-PEE-tray*
▶**Q**
queso *KAY-so*
quiosco de periódicos *kee-OHS-ko deh
  pair-ee-OH-dee-kohs*
▶**R**
radio *RAH-dee-o*
rascacielo *rahs-kah-see-EHL-oh*
rastrillo *rahs-TREE-yo*
ratón *rah-TOHN*
redondo *reh-DOHN-doh*
regar las plantas *reh-GAR lahs
  PLAHN-tahs*
regla *REH-gla*
reír *ray-EER*
reloj (despertador) *reh-LOH
  (des-per-tah-DOR)*
remolque *reh-MOHL-kay*
repisa para libros *reh-PEE-sa PAH-ra
  LEE-brohs*
respiradero *res-pee-rah-DEH-ro*
restar *res-TAR*
restaurante *re-taow-RAHN-tay*
río *REE-o*
rodilla *roh-DEE-ya*
rojo *ROH-ho*
ropa interior *ROH-pah een-teh-ree-OR*
rosa *ROH-sa*
rosado *roh-SAH-doh*
rueda *roo-EH-da*
▶**S**
sábana *SAH-bah-na*
sacapuntas *sah-kah-POON-tas*
sala de estar *SAH-la deh es-TAR*
saltar a la cuerda *sahl-TAR ah lah
  KWER-da*
sal y la pimienta *sahl ee lah
  pee-MYEN-ta*
sandía *sahn-DEE-a*
sándwich *SAHN-dweech*
satélite *sah-TEH-lee-tay*
secarse el pelo *seh-KAR-say el PEH-lo*
seco *SEH-ko*
seis *sayce*
sendero *sehn-DEH-ro*
sentarse *sen-TAR-say*
serpiente *ser-pee-EN-tay*
servilleta *sair-vee-YEH-ta*
seta *SEH-ta*
siete *see-ET-tay*
silla (de jardín) *SEE-ya (deh har-DEEN)*
sobre *SOH-bray*
sobrina *soh-BREE-na*
sobrino *soh-BREE-no*
sol *sohl*
sombra *SOHM-bra*
sombrero *sohm-BRAIR-o*
sombrilla de jardín *sohm-BREE-ya deh
  har-DEEN*
sótano *SOH-tah-no*

subir las escaleras *soo-BEER lahs
  es-kah-LAIR-as*
sucio *SOO-see-o*
suéter *SWET-air*
sujetapapeles *soo-heh-tah-pah-PEHL-ess*
sumar *soo-MAR*
▶**T**
tambor *tahm-BOAR*
tarta de frutas *TAR-ta deh FROO-tas*
taxi *TAHK-si*
taza *TAH-sa*
tazón *tah-SONE*
techo *TEH-cho*
teclado *teh-KLAH-doh*
tejas *TEH-has*
tendedero *ten-deh-DEH-ro*
tendero *ten-DARE-oh*
tenedor *ten-eh-DOR*
terraza *teh-RRAH-sa*
tetera *teh-TEH-ra*
tía *TEE-a*
tienda de campaña *tee-EN-da deh kahm-
  PAHN-ya*
tienda de comestibles *tee-EN-da deh ko-
  mess-TEE-blehss*
tigre *TEE-gray*
tijeras *tee-HEH-ras*
tío *TEE-o*
toalla *toh-AH-ya*
tobillo *toh-BEE-yo*
tocadiscos *toh-kah-DEE-skoss*
tomate *toh-MAH-tay*
toronja *tor-OHN-ha*
torta *TOR-ta*
tortuga *tor-TOO-ga*
tostada *toh-STAH-da*
tostadora eléctrica *toh-stah-DOR-a
  el-EHK-tree-ka*
tractor *trahk-TOR*
tren *tren*
trepar *treh-PAR*
tres *trayce*
triciclo *tree-SEE-klo*
triste *TREE-stay*
trompa del elefante *TROM-pa del
  eh-leh-FAHN-tay*
trompeta *trohm-PEH-ta*
tucán *too-KAHN*
▶**U**
uña *OON-ya*
uno *OO-no*
uvas *OO-vas*
▶**V**
vaca *VAH-ka*
vacío *vah-SEE-o*
vaso de leche *VAH-soh deh LAY-chay*
velero *veh-LEH-ro*
vendedor de flores *ven-deh-DOR de
  FLOR-ess*
ventana *ven-TAHN-a*
verde *VER-day*
vestido *ves-TEE-doh*
violeta *vee-oh-LEH-ta*
▶**WXYZ**
windsurf *WEEN-soorf*
yogur *yoh-GOOR*
zanahoria *sah-nah-OH-ree-a*
zapatos (deportivos) *sah-PAH-tohs
  (deh-por-TEE-vohs)*
zoológico *soh-oh-LOH-hee-ko*
zorrino *soh-RREE-no*